Ketogenic Vegetarian C

Healthy Ketogenic Diet Vegetarian Recipes For Burning Fat

Copyright ©

Disclaimer

All the material contained in this book is provided for educational and informational purposes only. No responsibility can be taken for any results or outcomes resulting from the use of this material.

While every attempt has been made to provide information that is both accurate and effective, the author does not assume any responsibility for the accuracy or use/misuse of this information.

You should always consult a doctor regarding any medical conditions, the information in this book is not intended to diagnose or treat any medical condition or illness.

Table of Contents

Introduction

The ketogenic diet has been proven to be one of the best diets for losing weight quickly. The basics of the ketogenic diet are focused on consuming healthy fats in your diet and avoiding carbohydrates and sugars. Many studies show that consuming more carbs leads to more weight gain and obesity. The recipes in this cookbook are all low in carbohydrates, and high in fat, which is great for losing weight. This ketogenic vegetarian cookbook contains delicious recipes for all meals of the day, that do not include any meat.

If you are a vegetarian on the ketogenic diet, you may have a hard time finding good ketogenic recipes, since meats are high in fat. I have hand picked my favorite ketogenic recipes that do not include meat, and I would like to share them with you. Good luck and we hope you enjoy these delicious ketogenic vegetarian recipes for helping you burn fat and lose weight!

Chapter 1: Ketogenic Vegetarian Breakfast Recipes

Goat Cheese Keto Omelet

Ingredients

2 tablespoons olive oil

3 eggs, beaten

1 tablespoon crumbled goat cheese, or to taste

2 teaspoons chopped chives, divided, or to taste

sea salt and ground black pepper to taste

Directions

Heat olive oil in a large skillet over medium heat, swirling oil to coat the skillet. Pour eggs into hot skillet; eggs will bubble and firm immediately.

Lift cooked edges of the omelet with a rubber spatula and tilt the skillet so that the uncooked egg runs underneath the lifted edge. Continue cooking, lifting edges and tilting the skillet, until omelet is almost completely set, 1 to 2 minutes total cooking time; remove from heat. Spread out any runny egg evenly on the top of the omelet with a rubber spatula.

Sprinkle goat cheese, 1 1/2 teaspoons chives, sea salt, and black pepper over omelet. Gently lift one edge and fold 1/3 of the omelet into the center over the cheese and chives. Fold the opposite 1/3 of the omelet into the center.

Slide omelet to the edge of the skillet and flip, folded side down, onto a plate. Top with remaining chives.

Nutrition: 479 calories; 44 g fat; 1.4 g carbohydrates; 20.5 g protein; per recipe

Curry Pepper Omelet

Ingredients

1 tablespoon light sesame oil

1/2 teaspoon minced garlic

2 tablespoons minced onion

2 tablespoons thinly sliced green onion

1/4 cup diced red bell pepper

1/4 teaspoon salt

1/2 teaspoon ground coriander

1/2 teaspoon ground cumin

1/2 teaspoon ground turmeric

2 eggs, beaten

Directions

Heat sesame oil in a skillet over medium heat. Stir in the garlic, and cook for 20 seconds until fragrant, then stir in the onion, green onion, bell pepper, and salt.

Cook for a minute or two until the vegetables soften. Sprinkle with coriander, cumin, and turmeric; cook for 30 seconds until fragrant.

Spread the vegetables evenly over the bottom of the skillet. Pour in egg, and cook gently until set, then turn over, and cook for an addition 30 seconds to firm. Roll omelet onto a plate to serve.

Nutrition: 315 calories; 26.3 g fat; 8 g carbohydrates; 11.9 g protein; per recipe

Ketogenic Buttermilk Pancakes

Ingredients

1/2 cup coconut flour

1 1/2 tablespoons erythritol

1 tablespoon oat fiber

1/2 teaspoon gluten-free baking powder

1/4 teaspoon xanthan gum

1 pinch salt

1 teaspoon oil, or as desired

5 large eggs

1/2 cup butter, melted

3 tablespoons water

3 tablespoons heavy whipping cream

1 teaspoon cider vinegar

1 teaspoon vanilla extract

Directions

Whisk coconut flour, erythritol, oat fiber, baking powder, xanthan gum, and salt together in a bowl, breaking up any lumps in the coconut flour.

Preheat a griddle or pan over medium-low heat and lightly oil the surface.

Mix eggs, butter, water, cream, vinegar, and vanilla extract into the bowl with the coconut flour mixture. Stir well to combine; batter will be thicker than regular pancake batter.

Scoop 1/4 cup batter at a time onto the preheated griddle, leaving space between each pancake and smoothing the tops slightly. Cook until bubbles form, edges begin to dry, and the bottom is browned, 2 to 5 minutes.

Flip pancakes carefully using a thin spatula; continue cooking until firm and browned on the second side, about 1 minute more.

Nutrition: 110 calories; 10.8 g fat; 2.7 g carbohydrates; 2.7 g protein; per 1/12 of recipe

Cheesy Baked Omelet

Ingredients

8 eggs

1 cup milk

1/2 teaspoon seasoning salt

1/2 cup shredded Cheddar cheese

1/2 cup shredded mozzarella cheese

1 tablespoon dried minced onion

Directions

Preheat oven to 350 degrees F (175 degrees C). Grease one 8x8 inch casserole dish and set aside.

Beat together the eggs and milk. Add seasoning salt, Cheddar cheese, Mozzarella cheese and minced onion. Pour into prepared casserole dish.

Bake uncovered at 350 F (175 degrees C) for 40 to 45 minutes.

Nutrition: 314 calories; 21.2 g fat; 5.9 g carbohydrates; 24.8 g protein; per 1/4 of recipe

Mediterranean Feta Cheese Keto Omelet

Ingredients

2 tablespoons olive oil

6 spears fresh asparagus, trimmed and chopped

1/2 red bell pepper, chopped

1/2 cup cherry tomatoes, halved

1/2 cup chopped fresh spinach

1/2 teaspoon minced garlic

1/2 teaspoon dried oregano

1/2 teaspoon dried basil

salt to taste

2 tablespoons butter

6 large eggs

1/4 cup whole milk

1/2 cup crumbled feta cheese

1/4 cup shredded Cheddar cheese

Directions

Heat olive oil in a large skillet over medium heat; cook and stir asparagus and red bell pepper until the vegetables start to soften, about 3 minutes.

Stir in cherry tomatoes, spinach, garlic, oregano, basil, and salt and continue cooking until tomatoes are soft and spinach has cooked down, another 3 to 5 minutes. Remove from heat and transfer vegetables to a plate.

Melt butter in clean skillet over medium heat. Whisk eggs and milk in a bowl and pour into hot butter, swirling skillet to cover entire bottom with egg mixture. Pull up an edge of the omelet with a spatula and tilt pan to allow unset egg to run underneath and cook; continue around pan, lifting omelet edge and tilting pan, until all the egg mixture is set. Sprinkle omelet with salt.

Spoon cooked asparagus mixture onto one side of the omelet and sprinkle with feta and Cheddar cheeses.

Gently fold half the omelet over the vegetables and cheese and press edges lightly to seal in the filling. Cook until filling is hot and Cheddar cheese has melted, 1 to 2 more minutes. Cut in slices to serve.

Nutrition: 321 calories; 27 g fat; 5.3 g carbohydrates; 15.5 g protein; per 1/4 of recipe

Blueberry Pancakes

Ingredients

2 egg yolks

2 egg whites

4 ounces cream cheese

1/2 cup blueberries, fresh

Granular Splenda (for topping)

Directions

In a small mixing bowl, soften the cream cheese in the microwave about 30 seconds. Separate the eggs, adding the yolks to the cream cheese. In another small mixing bowl, beat the egg whites until stiff. Beat the yolks and cream cheese until creamy. Fold yolks into the whites gently. Heat some oil in a large, non-stick skillet on medium heat.

Drop the batter by large spoonfuls into the hot oil. Immediately drop 6-7 blueberries on each pancake.

When browned on the bottom, flip over and cook until browned on the other side. Flip them back over before removing.

Repeat adding more oil to the pan as needed. Serve each with Splenda sprinkled over the top, if desired.

Nutrition: 196 calories; 17 g fat; 5 g carbohydrates; 7 g protein; per 1/3 of recipe

Cream Cheese And Chive Omelet

Ingredients

2 eggs

1 tablespoon milk

salt and ground black pepper to taste

3 tablespoons cream cheese, softened

2 tablespoons seeded and diced tomato

1 tablespoon chopped fresh chives

Directions

Whisk eggs, milk, salt, and pepper together in a bowl.

Heat a 6-inch nonstick skillet over medium heat; pour egg mixture into the hot skillet, tilting so egg mixture covers the entire bottom of skillet. Slowly cook egg mixture until set, 5 to 10 minutes.

Arrange small dollops of cream cheese onto half the omelet; sprinkle tomato and chives over cream cheese.

Fold omelet in half over the fillings. Remove skillet from heat and cover until cream cheese has softened, 2 to 3 minutes.

Nutrition: 260 calories; 20.8 g fat; 3.1 g carbohydrates; 15.6 g protein; per recipe

Keto Spinach Onion Quiche

Ingredients

Small onion, chopped, 2 1/2 ounces

1 tablespoon butter

10 ounces frozen chopped spinach, thawed drained well

5 eggs, beaten

1/4 teaspoon salt

1/8 teaspoon pepper

12 ounces muenster cheese, shredded

Directions

Sauté the onion in butter until tender. Add the spinach and cook until all the moisture has evaporated.

Put the cheese in a greased 9-10" pie plate. Add the spinach mixture and gently mix into the cheese.

Beat the salt and pepper into the eggs; pour evenly over the cheese and stir to combine all of the ingredients. Bake 350° for 30 minutes until set.

Nutrition: 303 calories; 23 g fat; 4 g carbohydrates; 20 g protein; per 1/6 of recipe

Almond Flour Scones

Ingredients

9 1/2 ounces almond flour

1/2 teaspoon salt

1/2 teaspoon baking soda

1/3 cup oil

1/4 cup sugar free syrup, vanilla flavor

2 large eggs

Directions

Mix the dry ingredients in a medium to large mixing bowl. Add the remaining ingredients and stir until a stiff dough forms.

Drop by 1/4 cup portions onto a baking sheet. Bake at 350F for 17-20 minutes until golden brown and firm to the touch.

Nutrition: 294 calories; 27 g fat; 7 g carbohydrates; 9 g protein; per 1/8 of recipe

Cinnamon Muffins

Ingredients

3 eggs

1/4 cup plus 2 tablespoons oil

1/4 cup sugar free syrup

2 tablespoons water

1 tablespoon vanilla

1 cup flax meal

1/2 teaspoon baking soda

1/2 teaspoon baking powder

2 tablespoons cinnamon

Directions

In a medium bowl, beat the eggs with a fork. With a fork or spoon, beat in the oil, syrup, water and vanilla.

In a small bowl, combine the remaining dry ingredients, then stir into the egg mixture. Let stand 5 minutes. Spoon into 12 well-greased muffin cups without paper liners.

Bake at 350F° 12-15 minutes, or until they are lightly browned and seem set to the touch. Remove from the tin at once to cooling rack.

Nutrition: 130 calories; 12 g fat; 4 g carbohydrates; 3 g protein; per 1/12 of recipe

Ketogenic Cream Cheese Breakfast Crepes

Ingredients

8 ounces cream cheese, softened

3 eggs

1 tablespoon granular Splenda

1/2 cup MiniCarb bake mix

1/2 teaspoon baking powder

1/4 cup heavy cream

1/2 cup water

Directions

In a medium bowl, beat the cream cheese with electric mixer until smooth. Add the eggs and beat until smooth. Add the Splenda, bake mix, baking powder and seasonings. Beat until smooth. Add the cream and water; blend well.

Spray a 9 or 10-inch nonstick skillet with cooking spray and heat over medium heat. Pour 1/4 cup of the batter into center of pan and immediately lift and rotate the pan quickly to swirl the batter into a 6-7 inch circle.

Cook until the underside is well set and lightly browned. Very gently pry up the edges with a pancake turner that has been sprayed with cooking spray, then very gently, but quickly, flip the crepe over.

Cook until the second side is lightly browned. Remove to a plate and cool.

Onion Mushroom Quiche

Ingredients

6 eggs

1 cup heavy cream

8 ounces Swiss cheese, shredded

4 ounces onion, chopped, 1 medium

1/2 pound fresh mushrooms, sliced

2 tablespoons butter

1/2 teaspoon salt

Dash pepper

Directions

Sauté the onion and mushrooms in butter until tender and slightly browned. Beat the eggs and cream with the salt and pepper. Put the cheese in the bottom of a greased pie plate.

Top the cheese with the mushrooms, then pour the egg mixture evenly over all. Bake at 350° for 35 minutes or until a knife inserted in the center comes out clean.

Nutrition: 402 calories; 34 g fat; 6 g carbohydrates; 19 g protein; per 1/6 of recipe

Coconut Flour Waffles

Ingredients

4 tablespoons butter, melted

6 large eggs

1/2 cup sugar free vanilla syrup

1/2 teaspoon salt

1/2 teaspoon baking powder

1/4 cup coconut flour

Directions

Put the butter in a medium bowl

Whisk in the remaining ingredients in the order given, blending well after each addition. Let stand for 5 minutes to allow the coconut flour to absorb some of the liquid.

Bake in a preheated waffle iron slowly pouring in enough batter to almost fill the grid. Bake until golden brown.

Gently remove from the waffle from the waffle iron.

Nutrition: 214 calories; 18 g fat; 5 g carbohydrates; 10 g protein; per waffle

Chapter 2: Ketogenic Vegetarian Soup Recipes

Creamy Ketogenic Tomato Soup

Ingredients

2 tablespoons butter

1/2 cup onion, 2 3/4 ounces

28 ounce can diced tomatoes, undrained

2 cups chicken broth

1 cup heavy cream

Salt and pepper, to taste

2 tablespoons parsley, minced, optional

Directions

In a 3-quart pot, sauté the onion in butter until tender. Add the tomatoes, with their liquid, and broth; bring to a boil. Simmer 5 minutes. Puree with a stick blender until smooth.

Stir in the cream and adjust the seasoning. Stir in the parsley and serve.

Nutrition: 180 calories; 15 g fat; 6 g carbohydrates; 4 g protein; per 1/6 of recipe

Cheddar Soup

Ingredients

1 teaspoon butter

3 cloves garlic, minced

2 1/2 cups vegetable broth

3 cups chopped broccoli

1 cup heavy whipping cream

3 cups shredded cheddar cheese

salt and ground black pepper to taste

Directions

Melt butter in a saucepan over medium heat. Cook garlic until tender, about 2 minutes. Add vegetable broth, heavy cream, and broccoli. Bring to a boil; simmer until broccoli is tender, about 15 minutes.

Add cheddar cheese gradually, stirring constantly, until completely melted. Season with salt and pepper.

Nutrition: 411 calories; 35 g fat; 7.4 g carbohydrates; 17.4 g protein; per 1/6 of recipe

Creamy Avocado Soup

Ingredients

1 stalk celery, chopped

1 tbsp butter

1 tbsp olive oil

1 cup chicken broth

1 cup water

1 ripe avocado

1/3 cup heavy cream

1 tsp curry powder

salt and pepper, to taste

Directions

Chop the whites of two green onions and celery. Sauté in butter and olive oil.

Add chicken broth and water, bring just to the boil. Add cream and curry. Using a blender, purée with peeled avocado. Salt and pepper to taste.

Nutrition: 150 calories; 14 g fat; 5 g carbohydrates; 2 g protein; per 1/6 of recipe

Broccoli And Onion Soup

Ingredients

1 large red onion

2 tbsp coconut oil

1 tbsp tamari sauce

2 cups of fresh broccoli florets

5 cups of water

1 cup of whipping cream

1 large tbsp chicken soup powder

Directions

Start with a saute of the red onions in coconut oil. Then add the water and broccoli. Cook for 10-12 minutes.

Puree the soup with a immersion blender. Add the whipping cream at the end and only on low heat. Serve hot.

Nutrition: 207 calories; 20 g fat; 7 g carbohydrates; 3 g protein; per 1/6 of recipe

Mushroom Spinach Soup

Ingredients

1 tablespoon butter

6 ounces fresh mushrooms, sliced

1 tablespoon onion, minced

1 clove garlic, minced

1/2 teaspoon salt

1/4 teaspoon pepper

2 1/2 cups beef broth

2 ounces fresh baby spinach, roughly chopped, about 4 cups loosely packed

1/2 cup heavy cream, room temperature

Directions

Sauté the mushrooms, onion, garlic and seasonings in butter in a large saucepan until lightly browned, 5 minutes. Add the broth and wine; cook on high heat until reduced by half, about 4 minutes. Remove from the heat and put half of the soup in a small, deep bowl.

Puree the soup in the bowl with a blender. Return the puree to the pot and heat until the soup is hot.

Stir in the spinach and cream; heat through for a minute and serve.

Nutrition: 317 calories; 28 g fat; 5 g carbohydrates; 8 g protein; per 1/2 of recipe

Parmesan Tomato Soup

Ingredients

2 cups heavy cream

3 cups diced tomatoes with juice

1 cup finely diced celery

1 cup finely diced carrots

1 tbsp fresh oregano or 1 tsp dried

4 cups chicken broth

1 cup parmesan cheese, freshly grated

1/4 tsp black pepper

1/4 cup vegetable oil

1 cup finely diced onions

4 tbsp fresh basil

1/2 bay leaf

1 tsp salt

Directions

Heat oil in 4 quart soup pot. Add celery, onions and carrots. Saute 5 minutes. Add basil, oregano, bay leaf, tomatoes, and chicken broth. Bring it to a boil, reduce heat and simmer until carrots are tender for 15 minutes.

Simmer, stirring constantly, until soup begins to thicken. Add Parmesan cheese and whisk to blend. Stir heavy cream, salt and pepper.

Simmer over low heat 15-20 minutes, stirring occasionally.

Nutrition: 289 calories; 26 g fat; 8 g carbohydrates; 8 g protein; per 1/8 of recipe

Cheesy Broccoli Soup

Ingredients

1 1/2 cup broccoli florets, steamed

4 oz cream cheese

1/2 cup heavy cream

1 1/2 cup chicken broth

1 cup cheddar cheese

Dash salt

Directions

Steam the broccoli until tender. Mix 1/2 cup of broccoli, all of cream cheese and all of cream in blender until smooth.

Pour mixture into a pot and add the rest of the ingredients, except the cheese. Heat over medium heat until it comes to a simmer.

Once heated, add the cheddar cheese and mix until melted completely.

Nutrition: 333 calories; 30 g fat; 5 g carbohydrates; 11 g protein; per 1/4 of recipe

Cream Cheese Artichoke Soup

Ingredients

1 tbsp celery, diced

1 tsp olive oil

1 cup chicken broth

1.5 cups heavy whipping cream

4 tbsp cream cheese with spinach and artichoke

2 cups cheddar cheese, shredded

Directions

Saute celery in olive oil until tender. Add chicken broth and simmer 5 minutes.

Whisk in heavy cream and cream cheese until smooth. Simmer 5 minutes, or until it starts to thicken.

Gradually whisk in cheddar cheese until smooth. Season with salt and pepper.

Nutrition: 583 calories; 56 g fat; 4.5 g carbohydrates; 17 g protein; per 1/4 of recipe

Mushroom Onion Soup

Ingredients

1/2 onion chopped

4 cups of mushrooms, chopped

1 clove garlic chopped

1 celery stalk chopped

2 cups chicken broth

4 tbsp of butter

Thyme and pepper to taste

Directions

Put butter in pot on medium heat. When melted add onion, garlic, and celery. Cooked until softened, add mushrooms, thyme and pepper.

Let cook for a few minutes then add chicken broth. Add water 2 cups of water. Let mixture heat on medium heat for about 15 minutes.

With blender, blend until desired consistency. Add in cream and blend.

Nutrition: 183 calories; 17.5 g fat; 5 g carbohydrates; 3 g protein; per 1/4 of recipe

Chapter 3: Ketogenic Vegetarian Main Dish Recipes

Eggplant Lasagna

Ingredients

2 eggplants

1/4 cup oil

2 cups low carb marinara sauce

16 ounces whole milk mozzarella cheese, shredded

1/2 cup parmesan cheese, grated

Salt

Directions

Trim the ends off the eggplants and slice lengthwise into 1/2" slices. You should get 6 slices from each eggplant. Brush both sides of the eggplant slices with oil to coat. Place them in a single layer on a baking sheet.

Broil about 5 minutes per side until tender and a little browned. Watch them closely because they can burn quickly. Lightly sprinkle them with salt after removing from the oven.

Layer everything in a greased 7x9x3" baking dish in this order: 4 eggplant slices, 1/3 of the sauce, 1/3 of the mozzarella.

Repeat the layering two more times then sprinkle with the parmesan cheese. Bake at 350F° for 30 minutes or until the cheese is bubbling.

Nutrition: 377 calories; 28 g fat; 9.5 g carbohydrates; 20 g protein; per 1/6 of recipe

Creamy Squash Bake

Ingredients

4 tablespoons butter

1 1/2 pounds yellow summer squash, sliced thin

Small onion, sliced or chopped

1 clove garlic, minced

1/2 teaspoon salt

1/2 teaspoon pepper

1/2 teaspoon Italian seasoning

1/4 cup fresh parsley, chopped

8 ounces Monterey jack cheese, shredded

2 eggs

1/4 cup heavy cream

2 teaspoons Dijon mustard

Directions

Sauté the squash, onion and garlic in the butter in a large skillet until tender and slightly browned. Sprinkle in the seasonings while cooking the squash.

Put the squash mixture in a greased 10-inch quiche pan; mix in the cheese and parsley. Whisk the eggs and cream in a small bowl; whisk in the mustard.

Pour the egg mixture over the squash; mix in gently. Bake at 375F° for 25 minutes. Let stand a few minutes before cutting.

Nutrition: 297 calories; 25 g fat; 4 g carbohydrates; 13 g protein; per 1/6 of recipe

Cheesy Parmesan Eggplant

Ingredients

1 pound eggplant

6 tablespoons tomato sauce

3 ounces mozzarella cheese, shredded

2 tablespoons Parmesan cheese, grated

Salt

Oil

Garlic powder

Directions

Slice the eggplant into about 12-13 thin slices. Salt both sides of each piece and place in a colandar in the sink for 30 minutes.

Pat dry with a towel and arrange on a greased, foil-lined baking sheet. Brush with oil and broil for a few minutes per side until slightly browned, oiling the other side after flipping.

Arrange 6 slices on the baking sheet; sprinkle with garlic powder and spread each with about 1/2 tablespoon of the tomato sauce. Top with a little mozzarella, then top each with another piece of eggplant.

Repeat toppings and finish with a sprinkle of parmesan on each. Bake at 350F° for about 10 minutes, until cheese is melted.

Nutrition: 113 calories; 9 g fat; 3 g carbohydrates; 5 g protein; per 1/6 of recipe

Scallion And Zucchini Frittata

Ingredients

2 tablespoons coconut oil, melted

1 cup shredded zucchini

1 small yellow onion, or to taste, grated

6 large eggs

1/2 cup almond flour

2 green onions, thinly sliced, or to taste

2 cloves garlic, minced

1 teaspoon onion powder

1 teaspoon dried basil

1 teaspoon sea salt

3/4 teaspoon freshly ground black pepper

Directions

Preheat oven to 350 degrees F (175 degrees C). Grease a baking dish with coconut oil.

Drain zucchini and onion in a colander until no longer wet, about 10 minutes.

Beat eggs, almond flour, green onions, garlic, onion powder, basil, sea salt, and black pepper together in a large mixing bowl until smooth; stir zucchini and onion into the egg. Pour the egg mixture into the prepared baking dish.

Bake in preheated oven until set in the center, 35 to 40 minutes.

Nutrition: 94 calories; 7 g fat; 2.5 g carbohydrates; 5 g protein; per 1/8 of recipe

Easy Cabbage And Egg Skillet

Ingredients

1 cup cooked cabbage

2 eggs

Butter

Salt and pepper

Directions

Melt a little butter in a medium skillet. Add the cabbage; stir and cook until hot.

Make a well in the center of the cabbage; break in the 2 eggs. Season. When almost done, mix the eggs into the cabbage.

Nutrition: 284 calories; 22 g fat; 5 g carbohydrates; 14 g protein; per recipe

Eggplant Mozzarella Casserole

Ingredients

1 eggplant, about 1 1/4 pounds before trimming

8 ounces mozzarella cheese, shredded

Breading mixture:

3/4 cup almond flour, 3 ounces

3/4 cup grated parmesan cheese, 3 ounces

1/2 teaspoon garlic powder

1/2 teaspoon Italian seasoning

Salt and pepper, to taste

2 eggs

Nonstick cooking spray

Directions
To make breading:

Combine all of the dry ingredients in a pie pan. Break the eggs into a cereal bowl and beat well with a fork. Position your oven rack in the center position. Preheat the broiler to 500F°.

Cut the eggplant into twelve slices of even thickness. Dip each piece of eggplant in egg to coat on both sides, then lightly coat them with parmesan-almond mixture.

Arrange the eggplant slices on a foil-lined baking sheet in a single layer. Spray the eggplant liberally with cooking spray. Broil about 3 minutes until golden brown; turn over, spray again with cooking spray and broil the other side. Watch it closely to prevent burning.

Spray an 8x8" baking pan with cooking spray. Arrange a layer of eggplant over the bottom of the pan, cutting them to fill the gaps.

Sprinkle half of the shredded cheese over the eggplant. Repeat layering eggplant and cheese.

Bake at 350F° about 20-30 minutes until the cheese is bubbly and golden brown on top. Cut into squares and serve with tomato sauce, if desired.

Nutrition: 465 calories; 34 g fat; 7 g carbohydrates; 30 g protein; per 1/4 of recipe

Green Chile Frittata

Ingredients

10 eggs, beaten

1/2 cup coconut flour

1 teaspoon baking powder

1 pinch salt

1 (7 ounce) can diced green chile peppers, drained

1 (16 ounce) container cottage cheese

1 cup shredded cheddar cheese

1/4 cup melted butter

Directions

Preheat oven to 400 F. Lightly grease a 9x13 inch baking dish.

In a large bowl, mix the eggs, flour, baking powder, and salt. Stir in the green chile peppers, cottage cheese, cheddar cheese, and melted butter. Pour into the prepared baking dish.

Bake 15 minutes in the preheated oven. Reduce heat to 325 F, and continue baking for 35 to 40 minutes. Cool slightly, and cut into small squares.

Nutrition: 225 calories; 16 g fat; 8 g carbohydrates; 16 g protein; per 1/10 of recipe

Artichoke Frittata

Ingredients

1/2 cup artichoke hearts, drained and chopped

1/2 cup chopped cherry tomatoes

1 (4.5 ounce) can sliced mushrooms, drained

6 eggs

1/3 cup milk

2 green onions, chopped

1 clove garlic, minced

1 teaspoon dried basil

1 teaspoon onion powder

1 teaspoon salt

ground black pepper to taste

1/3 cup grated Parmesan cheese

1 cup shredded mozzarella cheese

Directions

Preheat oven to 425 degrees F (220 degrees C). Grease a shallow 2-quart baking dish.

Heat a skillet over medium heat; cook and stir artichokes, tomatoes, and mushrooms until heated through, about 4 minutes. Transfer mixture to baking dish.

Whisk eggs, milk, green onions, garlic, basil, onion powder, salt, and black pepper in a large bowl; pour eggs over salami mixture. Sprinkle with mozzarella cheese and Parmesan cheese.

Bake until eggs are set and cheese is melted, about 20 minutes.

Nutrition: 211 calories; 14 g fat; 5 g carbohydrates; 17 g protein; per 1/6 of recipe

Squash Alfredo

Ingredients

2 cups cooked spaghetti squash

3 tbsp butter

3 tbsp cream cheese

1 clove garlic, crushed

1/4 cup grated Parmesan cheese

Directions

Using a knife poke through the squash several times and put it in the microwave on high for 12-15 minutes. Then slice it open, and scoop out and discard the seeds. With a fork scrape out the meat of the squash.

Stir all ingredients together and heat in microwave until the butter is melted.

Nutrition: 147 calories; 13 g fat; 5 g carbohydrates; 3 g protein; per 1/4 of recipe

Green Pepper Quiche

Ingredients

1 green pepper, cut in thin strips, 4 ounces

2 ounces onion, slivered

1-2 tablespoons butter

8 ounces Monterey jack cheese, shredded

6 eggs

1 cup heavy cream

1/2 teaspoon salt

Dash pepper

Directions

Sauté the peppers and onion in butter until tender. Place the cheese in a greased large pie plate. Top with the pepper mixture. Beat the eggs with the cream, salt and pepper.

Pour evenly over the peppers. Bake at 350F° 35 minutes, until a knife inserted in the center comes out clean.

Let stand 10 minutes before cutting.

Nutrition: 393 calories; 35 g fat; 4 g carbohydrates; 17 g protein; per 1/4 of recipe

Asparagus And Mushroom Frittata

Ingredients

1 tablespoon olive oil, or as needed

1/2 onion, chopped

1/2 red bell pepper, diced

4 button mushrooms, diced

1 stalk fresh asparagus, trimmed and chopped

6 egg whites

2 eggs

1/3 cup milk

1 cup shredded cheddar cheese

cooking spray

Directions

Preheat oven to 375 degrees F (190 degrees C). Spray an 8-inch square baking dish with cooking spray.

Heat olive oil in a skillet over medium heat; cook and stir onion, red bell pepper, mushrooms, and asparagus until onion is translucent, 5 to 10 minutes. Spread onion mixture into the prepared baking dish.

Beat egg whites, eggs, and skim milk together in a bowl until smooth; pour over onion mixture. Sprinkle Cheddar cheese over egg mixture.

Bake in the preheated oven until frittata is set in the middle and a fork inserted in the middle comes out clean, 20 to 25 minutes.

Nutrition: 226 calories; 15 g fat; 5 g carbohydrates; 17 g protein; per 1/4 of recipe

Mushroom Feta cheese Quiche

Ingredients

1 1/2 teaspoons olive oil

5 green onions, chopped

2 cloves garlic, finely chopped

1 (6 ounce) bag fresh baby spinach

1 1/2 teaspoons olive oil

8 fresh mushrooms, sliced

4 eggs

8 ounces sheep-milk feta cheese, crumbled

1 pound jalapeno yogurt cheese, shredded

Directions

Preheat oven to 325 degrees F (165 degrees C).

Heat 1 1/2 teaspoon olive oil in a nonstick oven-safe skillet over medium heat; cook and stir green onions and garlic in the hot oil until the garlic is fragrant but not browned, about 1 minute. Stir in spinach, cover skillet, and cook until spinach is wilted, about 5 minutes. Transfer spinach to a large bowl.

Heat 1 1/2 teaspoon olive oil in same skillet and turn heat to medium-high. Cook and stir mushrooms until lightly browned, about 5 minutes; remove from heat.

Squeeze any moisture from spinach mixture and stir into mushrooms. Beat eggs in a bowl until thoroughly combined. Stir eggs into the spinach-mushroom mixture; thoroughly stir in feta and jalapeno yogurt cheeses.

Spoon the mixture back into the skillet; use a spoon to level surface. Wipe any filling from edge of skillet above the filling with a paper towel.

Bake in the preheated oven until the quiche is golden brown, about 45 minutes. Let cool slightly before cutting into slices.

Nutrition: 342 calories; 26.7 g fat; 3.6 g carbohydrates; 20.7 g protein; per 1/8 of recipe

Printed in Great Britain
by Amazon